Food Chains and Webs

Ocean
Food Chains

Angela Royston

Raintree is an imprint of Capstone Global Library Limited, a company incorporated in England and Wales having its registered office at 7 Pilgrim Street, London, EC4V 6LB – Registered company number: 6695582

www.raintreepublishers.co.uk
myorders@raintreepublishers.co.uk

Edited by Claire Throp, Diyan Leake and Helen Cox Cannons
Designed by Joanna Malivoire and Philippa Jenkins
Original illustrations © Capstone Global Library Ltd 2014
Picture research by Elizabeth Alexander and Tracy Cummins
Production by Victoria Fitzgerald
Originated by Capstone Global Library Ltd
Printed and bound in China

ISBN 9781 4062 8416 4 (hardback)
18 17 16 15 14
10 9 8 7 6 5 4 3 2 1

ISBN 9781 4062 8423 2 (paperback)
19 18 17 16 15
10 9 8 7 6 5 4 3 2 1

British Library Cataloguing in Publication Data
A full catalogue record for this book is available from the British Library.

Acknowledgements
We would like to thank the following for permission to reproduce photographs: Alamy pp. 9, 17d (© National Geographic Image Collection), 10 (© Ron Chapple Stock), 11e, 17e (© Kelvin Aitken/VWPICS), 15 (© Dinodia Photos), 22 (© WaterFrame), 23b, 25 snapper (© David Fleetham); Corbis pp. 11b (© Norbert Wu/Minden Pictures), 12 (© Visuals Unlimited), 19 (© Ralph Lee Hopkins); FLPA p. 17c (Norbert Wu/Minden Pictures); Getty Images pp. 14 (Paul Souders), 23d, 25 coral (Oxford Scientific); Shutterstock pp. 1 (© Vlad61), 4 (© tororo reaction), 5 (© cdelacy), 7, 13, 29 (© Ethan Daniels), 8 (© BigRoloImages), 11a (© aldorado), 11c (© Leonardo Gonzalez), 11d (© Lebendkulturen.de), 16 (© Incredible Arctic), 17a (© qingqing), 17b (© AleksandrN), 18 (© Dray van Beeck), 20 (© BioLife Pics), 21 (© Solodov Alexey), 23a, 23c, 25 butterfly fish, 25 shark (© Greg Amptman), 24, 25 turtle (© Isabelle Kuehn), 25 parrotfish (© stephan kerkhofs), 25 seagrass (© Rich Carey), 25 seaweed (© iofoto), 27 (© Mark Medcalf), 28 (© kolyvanov); Superstock p. 26 (age fotostock).

Cover photograph of a green turtle eating a red jellyfish reproduced with permission of Getty Images (© Ai Angel Gentel).

We would like to thank Michael Bright for his invaluable help in the preparation of this book.

Every effort has been made to contact copyright holders of material reproduced in this book. Any omissions will be rectified in subsequent printings if notice is given to the publisher.

Contents

Some words are shown in bold, **like this.**
You can find out what they mean by
looking in the glossary.

Living in the oceans

Oceans may look bare, but under the surface is an amazing living world. Most sea animals live in shallow water around the coasts, but some live in deep water further out to sea.

Oceans are huge and deep, except close to the coasts.

A great white shark feeds on seals, fishes and even other sharks.

Sea animals include tiny shrimps, fishes and huge whales. This book looks at what they eat and how they survive.

Where are the oceans?

The map below gives the names of the different oceans in the world. The coldest waters are in the Arctic and Southern Oceans. The warmest waters are on each side of the Equator.

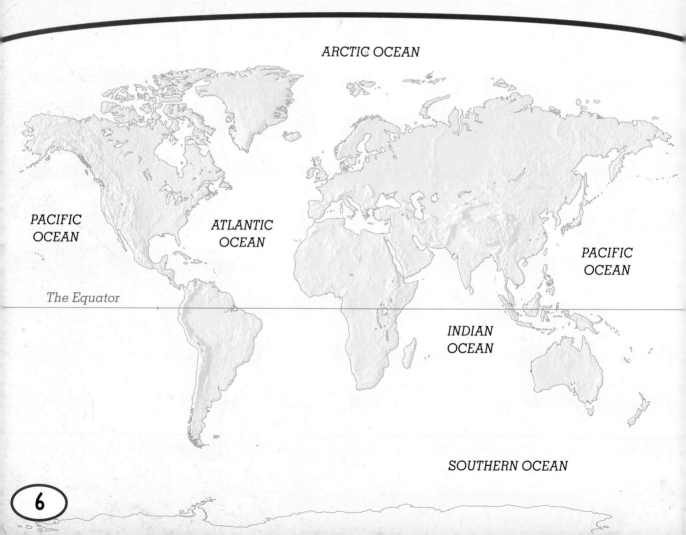

ARCTIC OCEAN

PACIFIC
OCEAN

ATLANTIC
OCEAN

PACIFIC
OCEAN

The Equator

INDIAN
OCEAN

SOUTHERN OCEAN

World's largest ocean

The Pacific Ocean covers a larger area than all the **continents** put together.

Coral reefs are home to millions of sea animals.

What is a food chain?

All living things need food to survive. Food gives them **energy** to live, grow and move.

Penguins use their wings to swim and to keep their balance.

Krill swim together in large groups.

A **food chain** shows how the energy in food passes from one living thing to another. For example, when a penguin eats **krill**, the penguin's body breaks down the krill to get energy.

An Atlantic food chain

The **food chain** opposite is from the
Atlantic coast of North America. It shows
how **energy** passes from microscopic
plankton through tiny animals called
copepods to herring. It then passes to squid
and, finally, a dolphin.

This is the Atlantic
Ocean, off Florida, USA.

Food chain

A dolphin feeds on a squid

A squid catches a herring

A herring feeds on a copepod

A copepod feeds on plankton

Plankton is made up of tiny living things

Where do food chains begin?

Ocean **food chains** begin with **plankton**. Plankton is made up of tiny animals and plant-like living things that float near the surface of the water.

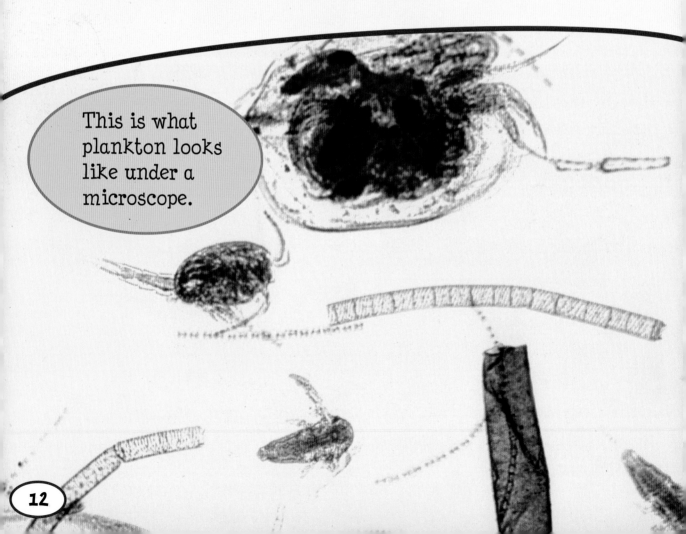

This is what plankton looks like under a microscope.

Seaweed is a type of **alga**, which also makes its own food.

The tiny plant-like living things are called phytoplankton and they use the **energy** of sunlight to make their own food. The tiny animals are called zooplankton and they feed on the plants.

Sea animals

Many kinds of sea animals feed on **plankton**. They include jellyfish and **krill**. The Blue whale is the largest animal that has ever lived and it feeds on huge amounts of krill and **copepods.**

A jellyfish floats through the water.

Big fish, such as
these tuna, feed on
smaller fish.

Animals that feed on other animals
are called **carnivores**. Large
carnivores, such as tuna fish, hunt
many types of smaller fish, including
shoals of young bluefish.

An Arctic food chain

Some sea animals live in the icy waters near the Arctic and Antarctic. This is an Arctic **food chain**. It shows how **energy** passes from the **plankton** through the **krill** to the cod. It then passes to the seal and on to the killer whale.

The icy Arctic Ocean

Food chain

A killer whale catches a seal

A seal feeds on a cod

A cod swallows tiny krill

Krill feed on plankton

Phytoplankton provide food for krill

Top predators

A killer whale is at the top of the Arctic **food chain**. No ocean animal dares to attack it. Some sharks, such as mako sharks, are among top **predators** in other oceans.

A blue shark is a top predator in cool and tropical seas.

A polar bear is a top predator in its food chain.

There are fewer top predators than other sea animals. Each link in a food chain needs lots of **prey** in the link below it to survive.

Living off the remains

Some **predators** are also **scavengers**, which means that they feed off the remains of dead animals.

This coral crab lives in the Caribbean Sea.

Amphipods are scavengers. They look for remains at the bottom of oceans.

Crabs, lobsters and many other animals that live at the bottom of the oceans are scavengers. They eat the remains of dead animals that sink to the seabed. These animals help to recycle waste.

Coral reef food chain

About a quarter of all known types of sea animals live around coral reefs. The coral reef itself is made by tiny animals called **coral polyps.** The **food chain** opposite is of a coral reef in Hawaii.

Coral polyps stick together to form a rocky coral reef.

Food chain

A tiger shark is a top **predator**. It preys on a snapper.

A snapper catches a young butterfly fish.

A butterfly fish feeds on the coral polyps.

Plankton that live inside coral polyps provide the polyps with food.

Food webs

A **food web** shows how different **food chains** link together. The food web opposite shows how some sea animals on the coral reef compete for the same food, and may be in danger from several **predators**.

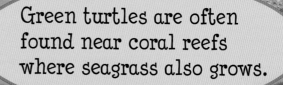

Green turtles are often found near coral reefs where seagrass also grows.

Food web

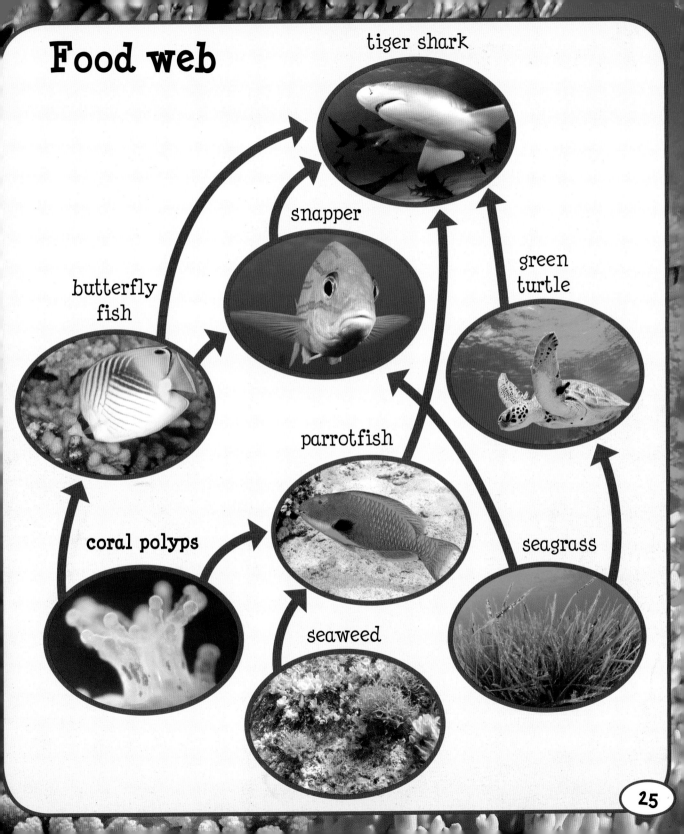

tiger shark

snapper

butterfly fish

green turtle

parrotfish

coral polyps

seagrass

seaweed

Broken chains

When one part of a **food chain** is damaged, the whole chain can break down. Many fish and sea birds feed on sand eels. However sand eels are becoming scarce in the North Atlantic, mainly because people are catching too many of them.

Sand eels are food for many ocean animals.

Puffins feed their young on sand eels.

It is now harder for animals higher up the North Atlantic food chain, such as puffins, to survive.

Protecting food chains

Many **food chains** are in danger of breaking down. One reason is that huge fishing trawlers are catching too many fish and destroying ocean **habitats**.

Fishing trawlers take huge amounts of fish from the sea.

Coral reefs die when the water around them becomes too warm. If the coral dies, other sea animals cannot survive there either.

One solution is to make marine reserves. These are areas of ocean where fishing is banned.

Glossary

alga tiny living thing, for example, green slime. Algae can make their own food.

carnivore animal that eats only the meat of other animals

continent large area of land

copepod tiny creature similar to a water flea

coral polyp small sea animal that sticks together in clumps. Some types of polyp build stony "houses", one on top of the other, to form a hard coral reef.

energy power needed to do something, such as move, breathe or swallow

food chain diagram that shows how energy passes from plants to different animals

food web diagram that shows how different plants and animals in a habitat are linked by what they eat

habitat place where something lives

krill tiny shrimp that feeds on plankton

plankton tiny animals and plant-like living things that float near the surface of water

predator animal that hunts other animals for food

prey animal hunted for food

scavenger animal that feeds off the flesh and remains of dead animals

Find out more

Books

Food Chains (Cycles in Nature), Theresa Greenaway (Wayland, 2014)

Ocean (Life Cycles), Sean Callery (Kingfisher, 2012)

Ocean Food Chains (Protecting Food Chains), Heidi Moore (Raintree, 2010)

Who Eats Who at the Seashore? (Food Chains in Action), Moira Butterfield (Franklin Watts, 2009)

Websites

www.greatbarrierreef.com.au/information/great-barrier-reef-food-web
Find out about food chains and a food web on Australia's Great Barrier Reef from this informative website.

kids.nationalgeographic.co.uk/kids/activities/new/ocean
This website includes videos, games and photos as well as information about the oceans.

www.nhm.ac.uk/kids-only/life/life-sea/index.html
This section of the Natural History Museum's website includes amazing information about giant squids, sharks and other fascinating sea creatures.

Index